MORE DISNEY SONGS FOR CLASSICAL PIANO

CONTENTS

Cover photo © Disney Enterprises, Inc.

The following songs are the property of:
Bourne Co.
Music Publishers
5 West 37th Street
New York, NY   10018

HEIGH-HO
PINK ELEPHANTS ON PARADE
SOME DAY MY PRINCE WILL COME
WHEN YOU WISH UPON A STAR

— PIANO LEVEL —
LATE INTERMEDIATE/EARLY ADVANCED

ISBN 978-1-61780-600-1

HAL•LEONARD®
CORPORATION

7777 W. BLUEMOUND RD. P.O. BOX 13819 MILWAUKEE, WI 53213

Visit Hal Leonard Online at
www.halleonard.com

Visit Phillip at
www.phillipkeveren.com

BAROQUE HOEDOWN

from MAIN STREET ELECTRICAL PARADE
at Disneyland Park and Magic Kingdom Park

By JEAN JACQUES PERREY
and GERSHON KINGSLEY
Arranged by Phillip Keveren

Spirited (♩ = 88–92)

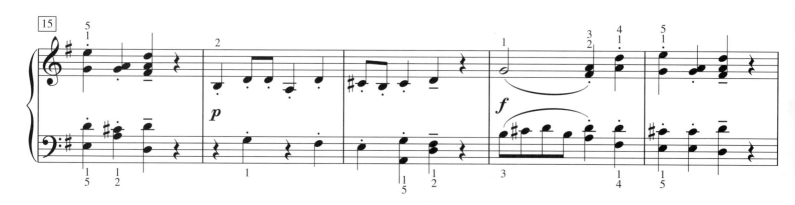

BE OUR GUEST
from Walt Disney's BEAUTY AND THE BEAST

Lyrics by HOWARD ASHMAN
Music by ALAN MENKEN
Arranged by Phillip Keveren

BELLA NOTTE
(This Is the Night)
from Walt Disney's LADY AND THE TRAMP

Words and Music by PEGGY LEE
and SONNY BURKE
Arranged by Phillip Keveren

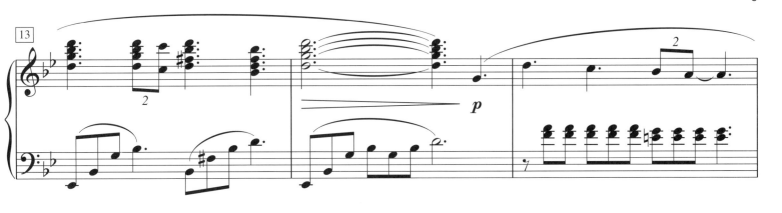

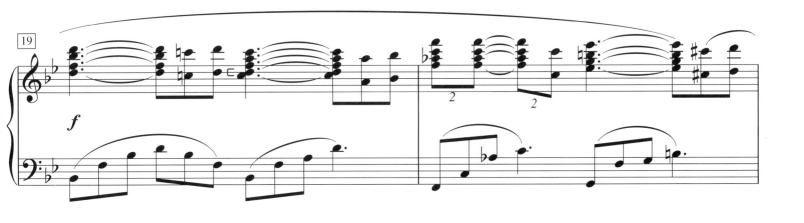

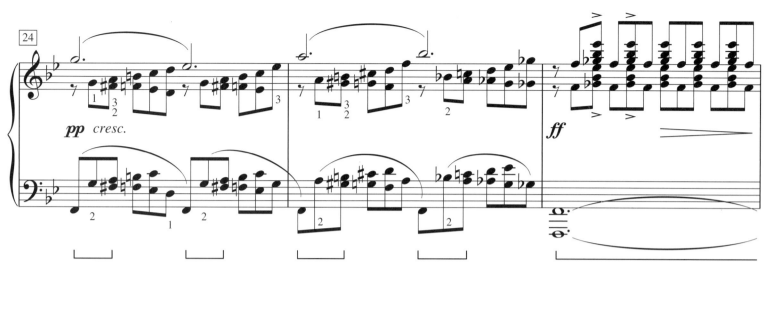

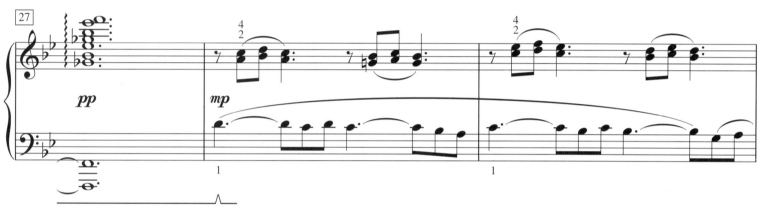

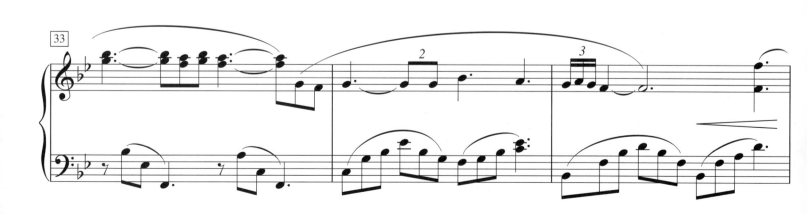

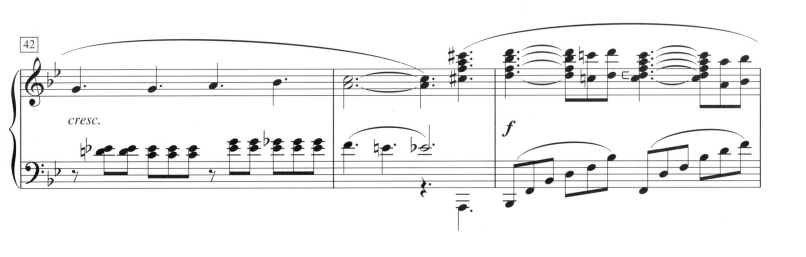

THE BELLS OF NOTRE DAME

from Walt Disney's THE HUNCHBACK OF NOTRE DAME

Music by ALAN MENKEN
Lyrics by STEPHEN SCHWARTZ
Arranged by Phillip Keveren

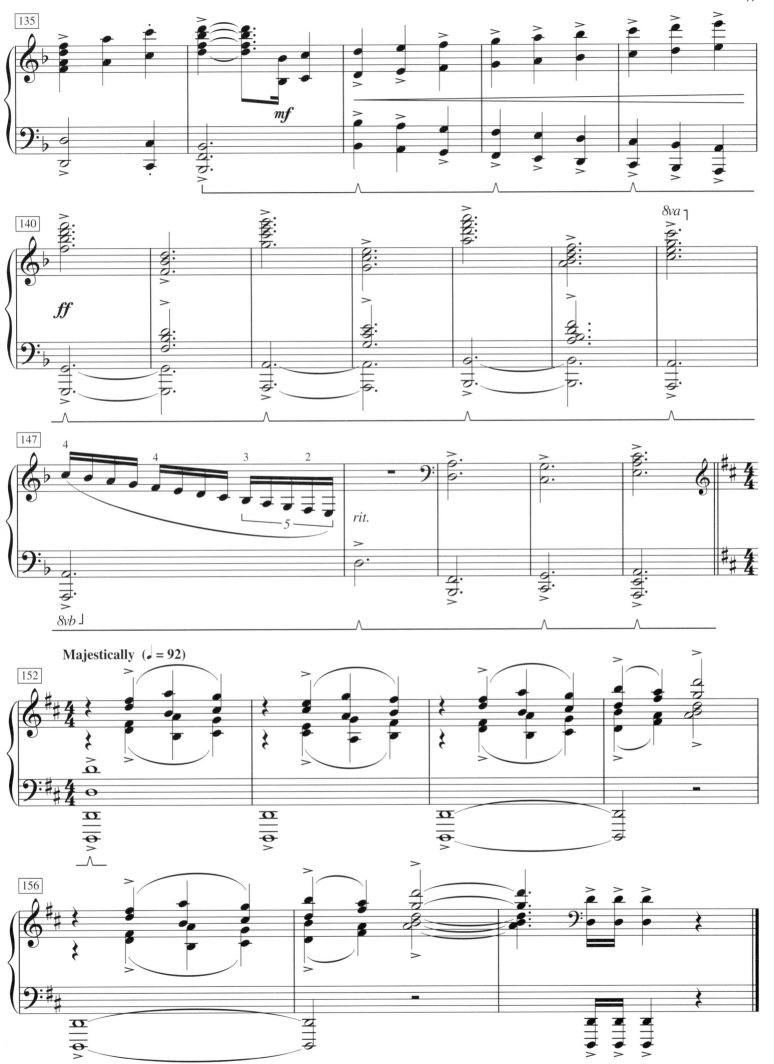

FEED THE BIRDS
from Walt Disney's MARY POPPINS

Words and Music by RICHARD M. SHERMAN
and ROBERT B. SHERMAN
Arranged by Phillip Keveren

FOLLOWING THE LEADER
from Walt Disney's PETER PAN

Words by TED SEARS and WINSTON HIBLER
Music by OLIVER WALLACE
Arranged by Phillip Keveren

HEIGH-HO

The Dwarfs' Marching Song from Walt Disney's SNOW WHITE AND THE SEVEN DWARFS

Words by LARRY MOREY
Music by FRANK CHURCHILL
Arranged by Phillip Keveren

Allegretto grazioso (♩ = 104)

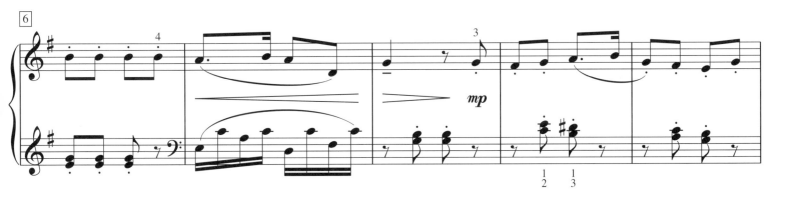

LOVE IS A SONG
from Walt Disney's BAMBI

Words by LARRY MOREY
Music by FRANK CHURCHILL
Arranged by Phillip Keveren

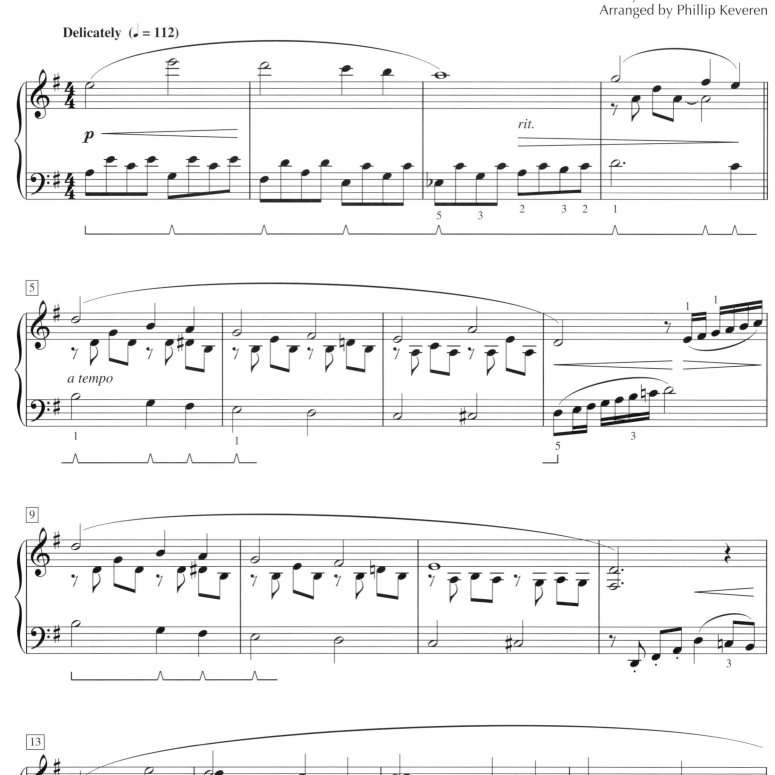

Tempo I (♩ = 112)

PART OF YOUR WORLD
from Walt Disney's THE LITTLE MERMAID

Music by ALAN MENKEN
Lyrics by HOWARD ASHMAN
Arranged by Phillip Keveren

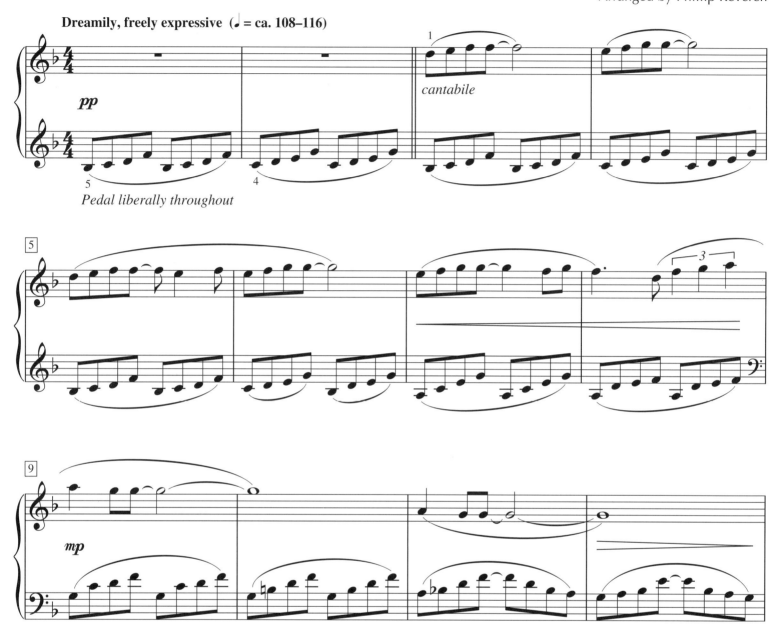

PINK ELEPHANTS ON PARADE
from Walt Disney's DUMBO

Words by NED WASHINGTON
Music by OLIVER WALLACE
Arranged by Phillip Keveren

Briskly, yet ponderously (♩. = 120)

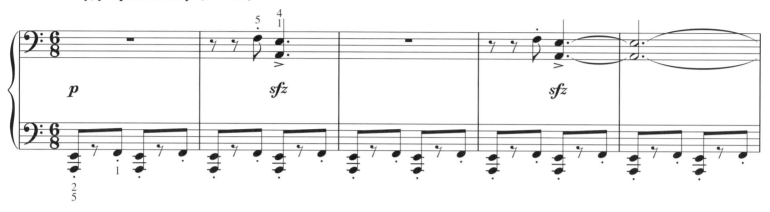

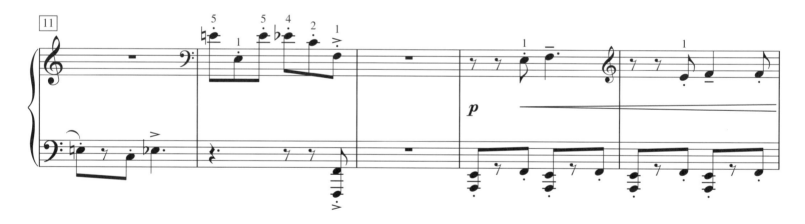

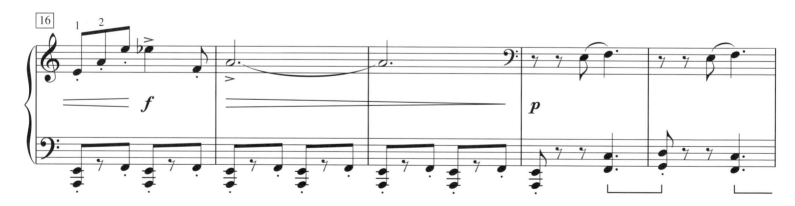

RATATOUILLE MAIN THEME
from Walt Disney Pictures' RATATOUILLE – A Pixar Film

Music by MICHAEL GIACCHINO
Arranged by Phillip Keveren

Tempo I (♩ = 100)

SOME DAY MY PRINCE WILL COME

from Walt Disney's SNOW WHITE AND THE SEVEN DWARFS

Words by LARRY MOREY
Music by FRANK CHURCHILL
Arranged by Phillip Keveren

SUPERCALIFRAGILISTICEXPIALIDOCIOUS

from Walt Disney's MARY POPPINS
Variations

Words and Music by RICHARD M. SHERMAN
and ROBERT B. SHERMAN
Arranged by Phillip Keveren

Brightly ($\quad$ = 120)

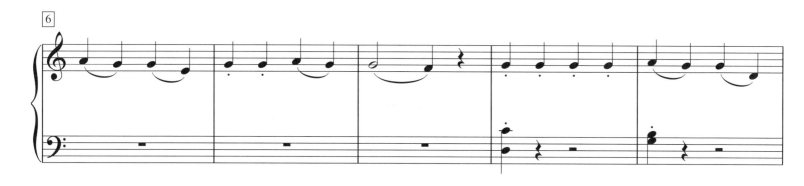

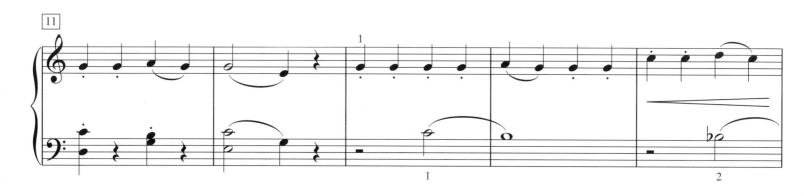

WHEN YOU WISH UPON A STAR
from Walt Disney's PINOCCHIO

Words by NED WASHINGTON
Music by LEIGH HARLINE
Arranged by Phillip Keveren

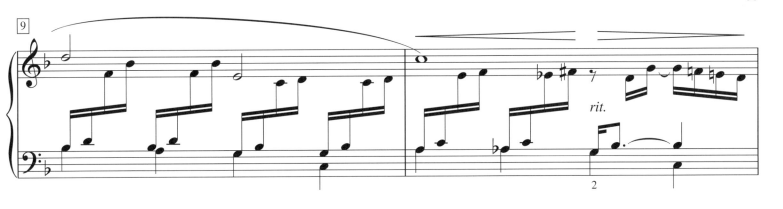

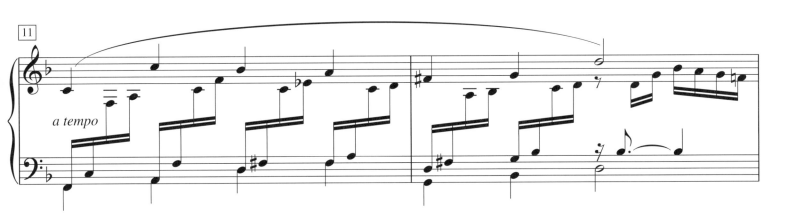

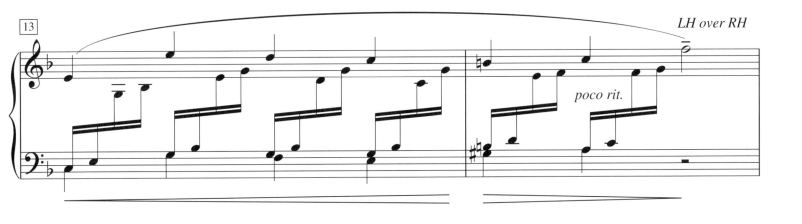

A WHOLE NEW WORLD

from Walt Disney's ALADDIN

Music by ALAN MENKEN
Lyrics by TIM RICE
Arranged by Phillip Keveren

ZIP-A-DEE-DOO-DAH
from Walt Disney's SONG OF THE SOUTH

Words by RAY GILBERT
Music by ALLIE WRUBEL
Arranged by Phillip Keveren

Tempo di marcia (♩ = 120)

ARRANGEMENT NOTES

Baroque Hoedown

This composition was featured in Disney's *Main Street Electrical Parade*. I have wonderful youthful memories of warm summer evenings in the Magic Kingdom watching this fascinating parade. The recording that accompanied the floats was all synthesizer-based, full of fantastic otherworldly sounds. This piano arrangement "is what it is"—a light-hearted nod toward the classical idiom.

Be Our Guest

This delightful tune from *Beauty and the Beast* gets the "Nutcracker" treatment in this incarnation. It is modeled after Pyotr Il'yich Tchaikovsky's "Trepak" from *The Nutcracker*, and will benefit from a brisk tempo and crisp articulation.

Bella Notte

This gem of a song from *Lady and the Tramp* is approached in a Romantic style reminiscent of Frédéric Chopin. In fact, Chopin's "Prelude in B-flat Major" (Opus 28, No. 21) is directly referenced in transition material beginning in measure 22.

The Bells of Notre Dame

From *The Hunchback of Notre Dame*, this arrangement should be played with dramatic flair. The setting draws stylistic inspiration from the piano works of Sergei Rachmaninoff.

Feed the Birds

Reportedly one of Walt Disney's favorite songs, this poignant song from the Sherman brothers is *simply* elegant. A tender waltz in A-B-A form, the B section is an improvisatory flight of fancy over the song's harmonic progression.

Following the Leader

The introduction of this arrangement is drawn from Felix Mendelssohn's "Jägerlied" (Op. 19b-3). The song, from *Peter Pan*, should be executed with scant pedaling and a strong two-beat pulse.

Heigh-Ho

Any number of Clementi sonatinas can be used as stylistic references for this arrangement. "Grazioso" is the key word here: *flowing gracefully*. Maintain a light touch, an approach that allows even the *forte* passages not to get heavy-handed. Let's not forget that this is a troupe of *dwarfs* heading off to work in the classic *Snow White*.

Love Is a Song

Robert Schumann provides the compositional template for this arrangement. Allow the melody to sing above the accompaniment, keeping the inner arpeggiated patterns light and steady. This is my favorite song from *Bambi*.

Part of Your World

Claude Debussy's "Rêverie" directly inspires this arrangement. Using the damper pedal liberally yet judiciously, one can create a dreamy underwater atmosphere that is perfectly appropriate for this song from *The Little Mermaid*.

Pink Elephants on Parade

Dumbo gave us this playful romp of a song. Béla Bartók's "Allegro Barbaro" inspired the arrangement. Careful attention to the dramatic dynamic changes will help bring this setting to life.

Ratatouille Main Theme

This bittersweet theme underscores the very clever animated film, *Ratatouille*. I have borrowed a portion of Chopin's "Mazurka in F# minor" (Op. 59, No.3) to serve as a B section in this setting.

Some Day My Prince Will Come

Truly one of the most beautifully constructed melodies in all of popular music, it transforms easily into a concert waltz for piano.

Supercalifragilisticexpialidocious

This buoyant melody provides wonderful material for a "theme and variations" treatment.

When You Wish Upon a Star

Felix Mendelssohn's "Lied ohne Worte" (Op. 19, No. 1) provides the inspiration for this arrangement. Mendelssohn's melody in his "song without words" has a soaring arc similar to this classic Disney song. To my ears, it seemed like a good stylistic pairing.

A Whole New World

Featured in *Aladdin*, this superlative melody fits nicely into the Romantic piano idiom. Eighth-note patterns in the right-hand melody against triplet figures in the left-hand accompaniment are a frequent feature in the music of Chopin and many other Romantic masters.

Zip-A-Dee-Doo-Dah

This carefree song is paired with stylistic elements from the music of Sergei Prokofiev, especially his piano work, "March" (Op. 65, No. 10). Keep a steady march tempo, accentuating the percussive nature of the instrument.